The Roles I've Played

A collection of scenes watched, heard, and lived

J. J. Gallmon

BookLeaf Publishing

India | USA | UK

Made with ❤ on the BookLeaf Publishing Platform
www.bookleafpub.in
www.bookleafpub.com

Dedication

For the ones I loved out loud,
the ones I loved in silence,
and the ones I wrote my way out of.

For whoever stayed in the audience
even after the lights came up.

Preface

Love arrives like opening night—
nervous, bright, and impossible to ignore.

These poems are what happens when the lights go down.
Every line is a memory, a conversation, or a rehearsal for
one that never happened.
I didn't plan to write a book about love.
I just started writing when silence became too loud.
Somewhere between the first confession and the last
apology, these poems appeared—
little monologues to people who may never hear them.
I wrote about falling in love, about trying again, about
leaving quietly,
about staying when I shouldn't, about the after.
This isn't a guide to love. It's the echo of it.
Together they build a play I never auditioned for but
couldn't stop performing.
So if you've ever confused being needed for being loved,
if you've ever stayed for the story instead of the ending,
if you've ever loved someone enough to let them leave—
welcome.
Lights — Go
Sound — Go
Curtains — Open

Acknowledgements

To *Familia and Bunny* —
for all the pieces shared and read.
Thank you.

To those who sat through my rewrites,
the ones who said, *"read it again, slower,"*
and the ones who simply said, *"I've been there."*

To the late-night drives,
and the playlists that made sense of them.
To the poets who taught me
that honesty can be a craft in and of itself —
Rudy Francisco, Ocean Vuong, Andrea Gibson —
and to every stranger who ever shared a story
that sounded like mine.

And to you —
for turning the page.
Thank you.

Act 1 Scene 1 . A Kind of Decanting

I love the way a glass touches a coaster—
a gentle touch,
a caress to signal my troubles will soon disappear.

I love the sound of chilled stones clashing against one another,
like the battle cry of a good time before it happens.
There has never been a greater drummer to sound for the troops.

I love the sight of whiskey being poured—
smoother than the jazz behind me,
tranquil like the first frost,
serene as an image on a postcard.
Polished.
Even.
Still.

I love the smell when I raise the glass—
the aroma so intoxicating my eyes start to roll,
exhilarating enough to raise chills on my skin,
enthralling to the point I almost dive headfirst.

I love the taste when it finally reaches my lips—
as my troubles burn away,
warmth spreading through me as it becomes one with
my veins,
peace washing over every ounce of my life.
A kind of decanting separating me from the world.
Nirvana.

But when I'm with you,
I lose all feeling in my knees
and every other part that should belong to me.
I can hear nothing but your voice as if it were a siren
song.
I see my entire life as if it were a prophecy of the future.
I smell the roses I've never stopped to acknowledge.

When I'm with you,
I can't taste my whiskey—
a kind of decanting separating us from the heavens and
the hells,
and everything in between.
Paradise.

Act 1 Scene 2. My Name Is...

You never told me your name,
and to be fair, I never said mine.

But with the exhilaration after every exhalation,
the spark in our eyes,
the lack of space between us—
...names didn't matter that night.

You said *I looked nervous*.
I told you *it's true*.
You asked me *why*.
I said *because of you*.

You leaned in closer.
I begged *not too close*.
You asked me *why*.
I said—

Because,
when you sit next to me,
every nerve suddenly stands at attention,
as if you were their general, ready to take any order you
mention.

Because,
with your voice this close to my ear,
I'm ready to make deals the devil would find hard to
accept,
just to keep the feeling of your breath on my neck.

Because,
if you were to move your hand on me,
I'm afraid you'd melt into my skin,
I'm afraid Medusa's power might be encased in your
fingertips,
I'm afraid you'll stop.

You moved in closer.
You took my hand.
You asked *if I was being honest.*
I whispered, *I'd take the stand.*

You started barking orders—
to make you scream,
to always say please.
You said *once we start I can't stop until you're finished
with me.*

You asked *if I want to leave,*
and before the words left your mouth,
I complied and said *please.*

I think we went back to my place.
If so, I wouldn't know it,
the way our clothes scattered the floor,
impossible to tell who owned it.

You still didn't ask my name,
and to be fair, I never said mine.

I think I told you *I loved you*.
I think I meant it that night.

Then you rolled your eyes
as I spelled out every reason why.

But as my lips pressed your skin,
as if they've always belonged there,
you pressed into me, leaving no space for a single
molecule of air.

I asked *if you trusted me to steer*.
You answered by *tightening your grip*,
running your hand through my beard,
the way you clutched the sheets,
spoke a lost language in my ear.

I think you might've been a gymnast—

5

the only way to explain
the way you bent like a straw,
how you could fold like a pretzel,
with every act making the climax that much more
suspenseful.

The room turned into a maze of angles and noise,
the walls cushioned our backs,
the floor broke our fall,
the table held us together,
we made the bed feel small.

Then your lips were on mine.
You still didn't ask my name.

You just whispered, *kiss me, hold me, show me I've
never been tamed.*

I think you told me *you loved me.*
I think I believed you that night.

I think sounds escaped,
decibels too high to read,
but even the night dared not interrupt us.
Waiting—if we'd ever come up to breathe,

watching—as lust formed tapestries,

in awe, at man and woman—
the world's first masterpiece.

We lived in bliss,
taught each other devotion,
croaked in rhapsody,
a lifecycle of emotions.

I don't think we were friends.
I don't think we were strangers.
I don't think we knew what came next.
I don't think we wanted to either.

In words unsaid,
I think we held one another
in some desperate plea
our bodies would write our names on each other.

Act 1 Scene 3. I'm Not Much of a Morning Person

I was never a morning person,
but now I don't sleep in past seven.

I never really cared for coffee or breakfast,
but after my morning workout I make sure to have my
hazelnut latte,
with a side of eggs cooked hard,
two strips of bacon,
and a blueberry muffin.

I never thought much of the color green,
but now I own three green ties,
five green shirts,
and today, to work, I wore one questionable pair of pants
in the same color.

I think salads are stupid,
but for lunch at least three times a week I'll have a
chicken Caesar with a side of fries—
...the fries are the most important part.

I don't watch too much baseball,
but this year I think the Jays have a real shot and I

already have season tickets.

I prefer to sleep with one pillow.
I've since learned that ten or twelve are just as
comfortable—
…but they can never cushion the space you left.

Before I met you
I wasn't much of a *mourning* person——
I guess people change.

Act 1 Scene 4 . I Wonder...

After every meal

I wonder if she'd like this?
I wonder if she'd prefer less salt
or more pepper?
I bet she wouldn't care for the sauce.

After every book I read

I wonder if she'd like this?
I wonder if chapter ten would piss her off
as much as it did me?
I bet she'd hate the character I loved.

After every movie I watch

I wonder if she'd like this?
I wonder if she'd think the pacing was a bit off?
I bet she'd notice the same cameos I did.

After every thought I have...

I wonder if she ate today?
I wonder what she's reading now?

I wonder if she watched anything new?
I wonder how she's doing?

I wonder if she wonders about me?
I bet she doesn't.

I bet she's happy——
I wonder what that's like?

Act 1 Scene 5. The Room Where It Happens

I thought a good education would open doors as I got older.

But with all my teachings combined,
I could never break into the mind of a woman.

I've dated women who seem to have thoughts secured in a room,
behind an ironclad tumbler,
equipped with voice recognition,
wrapped in vibranium chains,
encrypted by an enigma machine.

Every thought,
every decision,
every conclusion,
every resentment,
every commitment—
locked away.

And I... I wanna be in the room where it happens.

I've dated women who text me good morning,

while lying in bed with men they swore were devoid of
qualities only I possessed.

I've dated women who've ended entanglements over
breakfast,
with speeches that seemed prepared three months in
advance.

I've dated women whose tongues I could pick out of a
lineup,
but queries of future commitments were met with
laughter and promises of friendship

...I've loved a woman who I thought I would marry,
only to find our schoolyard promises buried in the
sandbox.

So, to the next woman I love—
...I wanna be,
I've got to be,
I beg to be,
in the room where it happens

Act 1 Scene 6. Anything But...

I don't know what to call it
when you reach for my hand, only when we walk alone.
I think you'd call it safety.

I don't know what to call it
when you call me at 2 a.m., because you can't sleep.
I think you'd call it boredom.

I don't know what to call it
when you lay in bed—my chest your pillow.
I think you'd call it comfort.

I don't know what to call it
when my heart beats like a drum as you snuggle in close.
I think you'd call a doctor.

I don't know what to call it
when I leave the party, because your name flashes on my
screen.
I think you'd call it reliable.

I don't know what to call it:
the way you feel like home.

I think you'd call it friendship.

I don't know what to call
the feeling of never wanting to let you go.

But I won't call it love—
I think...
I'm afraid you'd call it anything but.

Act 2 Scene 1. Theory

We never did have it easy.
It was one thing after another—
lack of communication,
either one of our mothers,
busy schedules,
or never seeing each other.

But do you remember
when you asked, looking deep in my eyes,
"Why is everything so hard when we do everything
right?"

And then,
to ease your mind,
I smiled and said,
"I have a theory."

I told you:
"There are an infinite number of universes where we
never end up together—
except *one*."

So that's how I know,
Somewhere, out there,

there's a me texting a you 'Good morning,'
so you know you're the first thought on his mind.
There's a me telling a you he loves you,
as if they're the only words he knows to be true.
There's a me telling a you he misses you
when you're right by his side.
There's a me saying 'Good night,'
patiently waiting for the sun to rise.
There's a me that knows a you to be his queen
while he plays your fool, your king.

Somewhere, out there,
there's a me who's your number one fan,
because you made him a better man.

And out there, somewhere,
there's a me that doesn't backspace every 'I love you'
text,
who isn't afraid of what you'll say next.
There's a me that doesn't bottle up everything inside,
using 'I'm alright' as a constant lie.
There's a me that doesn't have to fake a smile,
pretending he's fine.
There's a me that doesn't have this burning pain in his
chest,
who isn't the reason the links in our chain no longer
connect.

He doesn't live with a hole in his heart—
one he has to learn to accept.

There's a me that doesn't have a single regret,
because he still has *you.*

And then there's me—
I hate *him,*
but I wish you both the best.

Act 2 Scene 2 . Blueberries

My mother hates blueberries.

The smell makes her nauseous,
the texture leaves much to be desired,
the taste just doesn't suit her palate.

But no matter the occasion,
come hell or high water,
for some reason
if she sees one she'll eat it.

And sure enough,
whatever expression she wore beforehand
curls into a familiar disappointment.

But if you ask her why,
before she eats it,
she'll say,
"Who knows, maybe this time will be different."

I suppose that's why,
even though your lack of affection makes me nauseous,
your barren words leave much to be desired,
and I never quite seem to suit your palate,

no matter the occasion,
come hell or high water,

I'll choose you—
who knows, maybe this time will be different

Act 2 Scene 3. She Asked...

"Can we be honest?"
"Absolutely."

"Do you want to be here?"
"Not really."
"Why did you come?"
"My friends made me."
"Why did they make you?"
"Something about moving on."

"Do you want to move on?"
"Your eyes are beautiful."
"Are you lying?"
"No."
"Are you deflecting?"
"Absolutely."

She laughed.
I laughed.

"Why do you cover your mouth?"
"I hate my smile."
"You have a pretty smile."

I smiled.
I didn't cover my mouth.

"So, what's her name?"
"Don't you think that's more of a second date question?"

She laughed.
She had a pretty laugh.

"So do you have a he like I have a she?"
She did.
Not anymore.

"How did you move on?"
She paused.
"Time."
"Can I borrow your Time Machine?"

She laughed.
She had such a pretty laugh.

She asked about my job.
She asked about my friends.
I asked about her mom.
I asked about her dad.

She asked about my fears.

I asked about her loves.
She asked about my regrets.

I told her everything.
I don't know why I told her everything.

She listened.
She didn't leave.

I asked about her regrets.

She told me everything.
Why did she tell me everything?

I listened.
I didn't move a muscle.

She asked about her...
I asked about him...

We talked.
We laughed.
We cried.
We hugged.

"Will I see you again?"
She hugged me.

Longer.
Tighter.
She smiled.

I hugged her.
Longer.
Tighter.
I smiled.
"Of course."

We kissed.
She laughed.
She smiled.
"Liar."

Act 2 Scene 4. Philophilia by Night, Philophobic by Day

I owe you an apology.
I never told you—
I'm afraid of sleeping alone.

I told you beauty was synonymous with your name.
I told you your jokes scratched an itch I never knew I
had.
I told you my favorite color was whatever shade your
smile turned me into—
but I never told you it was blue.

I told you about my childhood dreams—
how I thought I could've gone pro.

I told you to tell me about your day,
to give me the overview
so that I could be the details.

I told you my hobbies—expanded when you leaned in
close to listen—
but I never told you I prefer to work out alone.

I owe you an apology.

I mistook company for closeness—
willingness for readiness.

I told you I would hold you through the night—
but I meant *just* the night.

I owe you an apology.
I'm afraid to sleep alone—
but terrified you'll be there in the morning.

I thought I'd learned to stay awake beside someone.

I'm sorry.
I was wrong.

Act 2 Scene 5. It's Been a Long Week

I love Fridays
Fridays are my best days
Fridays are my worst days
Fridays are my off days

I drink on Fridays,
because on **Mondays**
every promise we ever made repeats like a cursed record,
skipping when you said you'd stay.

I don't sleep much on Monday.

Throughout **Tuesday**
your laugh rings in my ear like an alarm—
I can never get it to snooze.

I don't sleep much on Tuesday.

I never call, but on **Wednesdays**
I dial your number
to see if my number's still saved,
to see if you still miss me,
to see if you've moved on yet.

I don't sleep much on Wednesday.

I wonder, on **Thursdays**,
what I could've done different... better.
What if I apologized that day?
What if I begged you to stay?
What if I loved you louder?
What if I loved you harder?
What if I loved you better?
What if we stayed just friends?

I don't sleep much on Thursday.

Ohhh but on **Fridays**,
on Fridays,
I drink.

I drink to skip over every promise we made,
I drink to silence your laugh,
I drink to blur your number on my phone,
I drink as if what if were a fifth.

I sleep on Friday.

Ohhh on **Fridays**,
I finally dream.

And there,
all our promises are kept.
I soak in your laugh,
I need not call because you're already with me,
I never have to wonder what if.

I always sleep on Friday.

Things go to shit on **Saturdays**.
I wake up.
I plead with the sandman for more time.
I don't move for hours,
and I can never get back to that dream,
no matter how much I drink.

I don't know if I sleep on Saturday.

Like clockwork, on **Sundays**,
I wake up.
I restock a cart full of medicine
to help me sleep.

I set it aside.
I lay down in bed.
And I cry,
because I know Monday is just ahead.

I don't sleep much on Sunday.

Act 2 Scene 6. How To Kill a God

Step One — Create the God

To do so: find another being similar to yourself.
Give your heart, your soul, your very being fully to one another.
Until the earth quakes, the skies shatter, hell freezes.
Then all that remains is a god.
You call it... love.

Step Two — Serve

You serve.
And you serve.
And you serve.
And you serve.

Until one day...

Step Three — Reject

You reject its teachings.
You start to wonder if things would be better if you did things your way
instead of our way.
You become selfish.

Step Four — Silence the Hymns

You stop reading the sacred texts — Partners.
You no longer sing the hymns — I love you.
The scripture loses its meaning — I love you too.
And finally...

Step Five — Death

To extinguish this god from existence,
to make sure it's dead and stays that way,
to turn it to myth, a fable, a fantasy tale that all who hear
will dismiss —
to kill a god...

You stop believing —
and tell yourself it never existed.

Act 3 Scene 1. Even Her

"Have you ever been in love?"

"...Once,...twice,...three times"

"You loved ###?"
"Utterly"
"And you loved ###?"
"Completely"
"Even ###?"
"Unquestionably"

"But after everything that's happened how...why?"
"Well...

I loved *her*
the way I wished I loved myself.
I loved her
so much that it hurts to breathe out her name.
I loved **her**
in a way that I still can't comprehend.

I loved *her*
because she believed I deserved to be loved.
I loved her

because she gave me a reason to smile.
I loved **her**
because she showed me that I could love again, that the first time wasn't a fluke.

I loved *her*
the way time and space exist—
inevitably.
I loved <u>her</u>
the way leaves change colors—naturally.
I loved **her**
the way an arrow pierces through a heart—painfully.

I loved *her*
because she is living proof angels do exist.
I loved <u>her</u>
because she brought peace to wars I didn't know I was fighting.
I loved **her**
because for a moment, I believed I was enough.

I loved *her*
more than anything that has or will exist.
I loved <u>her</u>
more than there are stars in the multiverse.
I loved **her**
more than all the movies said I would.

I loved *her*
because she's the reason I saw yesterday,
she was the reason the rope stays on the shelve,
she was the reason the toaster has never taken a bath,
she was the reason the knife's only home was a sheath,
she's the reason I'll see tomorrow.
She's the reason I am who I am today.

I loved <u>her</u>
because she was a home I never knew I needed,
she dragged me out of the abyss more times than I can count,
she believed that I mattered.
She's the reason I believe that I matter.

I loved **her**
because I still can't believe that I loved her,
it makes no sense how much I loved her,
it's senseless, the I way loved her,
love cannot explain why I loved her.
She's the type of love that only existed in fairytales
yet—she was my reality.

I loved *her*
More than I thought I could love.
I loved <u>her</u>

Even though I knew I shouldn't.
I loved **her**
In a way gods couldn't comprehend.

sometimes I wish I didn't,
sometimes I'm glad I did,
sometimes... I think maybe she loved me too

But even when I hate myself,
even when it hurts,
even when I can't comprehend why,
I'm grateful to have loved"

"Even her?"

"Even *her*."

Act 3 Scene 2 . Past Lives

In a past life, I'm sure they called us many things—

star-crossed.
ill-fated.
tragic.

I like to think we shared an equivocal alliance—
one that made just enough sense to us.

I wonder if all our lives were like this one?
Maybe we always fell apart.

No...
I think we're too stubborn to let fate decide that for us.

I bet we've been natural enemies,
I bet we've been friends of convenience,
I bet we've hated each other—
I bet we've been inseparable.

And in the lives we never met,
where our paths never crossed,
I bet it felt like something was missing.

So, at least once more—
in this life,
let's run into each other in a city—
amongst thousands.

We'll go for coffee.
We'll catch up—it's been ages.
We won't say goodbye.
We won't promise to meet again.

We'll just wait till the next life—
knowing this one's already in the past.

"Who do you think we are then?"

Act 3 Scene 3. Maybe One Day

One day I will figure out why
I am more comfortable with being
loved in silence.

Maybe
uncertainty brings me peace.

Maybe
ambiguity is my love language.

Maybe
because when you love me aloud,
I can't think of a reason you should.

Maybe one day,
I'll come up with one.

Act 3 Scene 4. I'm Fine

H ere lies the

E pitome of all I will forever

L ack.

P urpose, patience, passion.

M ettle, depth, optimism.

E ssentially, all that make us feel alive.

Act 4 Scene 1 . Thank you, Five

She's on her way up.
And I have five minutes
to remind myself we're just friends and nothing more.

Four minutes
to forget every romance plot that told me he was only
supposed to be a side character.

Three minutes
to kill the butterflies in my stomach,
left over from when we first met.

Two minutes
to scrub away the feeling of you in my arms—
I always miss a spot.

One minute
to come up with an excuse for why I just finished
showering,
but only my eyes are wet.

30 seconds
to remember how to smile.

15 seconds

to put together words that mean I'm happy for you.

10 seconds

to mean them.

I really want to mean them.

5...

4...

3...

2...

1...

Showtime.

Act 4 Scene 2 . Clouds

Clouds are made of water droplets.
Over time, the droplets condense and grow—
until they grow too heavy for the sky to hold.
It darkens,
and the droplets fall as rain.

This morning, sitting alone in my room,
listening to my usual collection of distractions,
the artist's voice lowers to a whisper,
and the melody begins to fade...

Suddenly, I'm angry.
I'm sad.
I'm confused.
I feel everything.
I feel nothing.
I feel everything.
I feel nothing.

And suddenly,
the inside of my abode becomes host to a storm.

Rain falls in what seems a never-ending downpour,
drenching my face,

soaking my shirt.

Suddenly thunder booms,
as if to shake the walls from their structure.
I scream.
I curse.
At nothing in particular.

Suddenly the wind reaches speeds Zeus would be proud
of.
Papers fly across the room.
Bottles crash against walls.
Pillows take to air,
as if they were Toto trying to reach Oz.

I didn't know how long this storm had been brewing.
I don't know how long it will last.

But suddenly,
my voice goes hoarse.
My eyes grow dry.
My arms tire.
Suddenly... the storm clears.

I think we're a lot like clouds—
born without asking,
and over time,

the very act of *being* condenses into a burden so heavy
sometimes,
it rains.

Act 4 Scene 3. Friends

No one told us life was gonna be this way.
That our love life was D.O.A.

That even if I loved you
more than Ross loved Rachel,
more than Rachel loved fashion,
more than Monica loved Chandler,
more than Chandler feared commitment,
more than Joey loved pizza,
more than Phoebe loved PETA—

some stories
don't end in lovers' amnesia.

But when the rain starts to pour,
like we've been there before,
I'll still be there for you,
knowing you'd be there for me too.

So, where Hollywood wrote a perfect end—
I'm grateful our story—
ended as *friends*.

Act 4 Scene 4. I Have Until June

They say a broken bone takes three months to mend,
and considering my chest caved in when you left me for
him...

Until June
I'll see you in my peripheral,
every time I open my eyes.

I'll let you consume every waking moment I have,
as if they always belonged to you.

I'll replay your laughter in my head,
pausing every time your smile comes to mind.

I'll forget I ever found beauty in another.

I'll freeze every time I hear your name,
biting my tongue to keep from calling it.

I'll continue to rush to sleep,
in hopes you'll appear in every episode of my dreams.

I'll let you occupy my heart,

as if you'd rented out the artery.

Until June...
In June...
I'll still love you.

They say a broken bone takes three months to mend—
I haven't come up with an excuse for a July yet.

Act 4 Scene 5. TV Remote

Growing up, I hated commercials—
those sudden interruptions
that came just when life was getting good.

Whenever one reared its ugly head,
I'd rush for the remote
I swore was just in my hand.

Even after I lifted every cushion,
checked under every surface my hand could squeeze in,
looked in both the freezer and the fridge,
and accused every contact in my phone
of somehow stealing the device,
it would never appear.

Then a funny thing would happen—
when I gave up,
resigning myself to the boring parts—
I kind of enjoyed it.

Freedom from finding the next best thing,
from remembering what I'd watched last,
from keeping up with a schedule I never made.

And just as I'd ceded the authority
the apparatus held over me—
it would reappear in my hand.

Love is a lot like that remote—
and I've grown tired of searching.

So instead,
I'll delete every app that boils down connection into two
cardinal directions—
freeing myself from monotony.
I'll delete all our old photos,
freeing myself of the past.
I'll delete the thought that I'm running too late,
freeing myself from a date that was never set.

Today I turned off the TV.
I went for a walk.
It was boring—
but I kind of enjoyed it.